THE GENTLENESS
OF THE VERY TALL

Linda France was born in 1958 in Newcastle. After living in Dorset, Leeds, London and Amsterdam, she returned to the North East in 1981, and now lives in Northumberland. She has two children and works as a freelance writer and part-time tutor in adult education.

She won the Basil Bunting Award in 1988 and 1989, and the Newcastle Brown Ale Poetry Competition in 1993. She was awarded the Arts Foundation's first Poetry Fellowship in 1993. She appeared in the ITV poetry series *Wordworks*, and in BBC 2's *On the Line* poetry special, *Ooh! Ah! Cantona!* She has worked on several collaborations with artists, including *Acknowledged Land* with Birtley Aris, and various public art commissions.

Her first collection, *Red*, was published by Bloodaxe Books in 1992. Her second, *The Gentleness of the Very Tall* (Bloodaxe Books, 1994), is a Poetry Book Society Recommendation. She is the editor of the Bloodaxe anthology *Sixty Women Poets* (1993), a Poetry Book Society Special Commendation.

Linda France

◊

THE GENTLENESS
OF THE
VERY TALL

BLOODAXE BOOKS

ISBN: 1 85224 287 6

First published 1994 by
Bloodaxe Books Ltd,
P.O. Box 1SN,
Newcastle upon Tyne NE99 1SN.

Bloodaxe Books Ltd acknowledges
the financial assistance of Northern Arts.

Cover printing by J. Thomson Colour Printers Ltd, Glasgow.

Printed in Great Britain by
Cromwell Press Ltd, Broughton Gifford, Melksham, Wiltshire.

For my mother
LILY FRANCE
1919-1994

Acknowledgements

Acknowledgements are due to the editors of the following publications in which some of these poems first appeared: *Bête Noire*, *Iron Erotica* (Iron Press, 1994), *Klaonica: poems for Bosnia* (Bloodaxe Books/*The Independent*, 1993), *Poetry Review*, *Poetry with an Edge* (Bloodaxe Books, new edition, 1993), *St Oswald's Hospice Anthology*, *Sunday Times*, *Tandem*, *Uncompromising Positions*, *What Poets Eat* (Foolscap, 1994) and *The Wide Skirt*. Some of the poems have been broadcast on various programmes on BBC Radio 3 and 4, and on BBC Television's *Look North*.

'Acknowledged Land' was commissioned by Graeme Rigby for *Northern Echo*'s *The Page* as a collaboration between Linda France and the artist Birtley Aris, and published in book form by Northumberland County Council in 1994. The poem spans 9000 years of Northumberland's prehistory, charting changes from the early Stone Age right through to the early Iron Age. The seven sections of thirteen couplets represent the diurnal (the days of the week) and the lunar (the moon months of the year).

'Her Father's Daughter' was an award winner in the Newcastle Brown Ale Poetry Competition in 1993, and 'Something for the Weekend' won first prize in the same competition in 1994. 'Everyman's Blues' was commissioned for Théâtre sans Frontière's programme of their 1994 production of *Notre Dame de Paris*, based on the novel by Victor Hugo; the poem is spoken, as one voice, by Esmeralda's admirers. 'Mae West on Furniture Polish' was part of Northern Stage's production of *Women Prefer* in 1992.

Linda France is grateful to Northern Arts for a writer's award given in 1992; to the Author's Foundation for an award made in 1993; to the Arts Foundation for their Poetry Fellowship for 1994; and to everyone at Border Wind for all their help.

Thanks are also due to James Adam, Auctioneers, of Dublin, for assistance with the cover painting, and to the Estate of Colin Middleton for their kind permission.

Contents

'Break a vase and the love that reassembles the fragments is stronger than that love which took its symmetry for granted when it was whole. The glue that fits the pieces is the sealing of its original shape.'

DEREK WALCOTT

'Courage and sex – that's what love is.'

from JANE CAMPION's *Sweetie*

Little Dogs Laugh

DOG was mongrel smile, stray and small as me,
pleated gums stitched with teeth. Kiss and lick
grew a bite, ripped open my playground lips.

Tears. Running red and mad barking
were muzzled by my sister's handkerchief,
a double-deck ride to the infirmary.

I blinked like a falling star, and sky
was the howl in my mouth. I wanted swings.
I wanted a cow to jump over the moon.

But little dogs laughing pinned me to a bed,
its whiskery blanket, with their crisp elbows,
a silver needle sewing the ragged corners.

I kicked. Back at home, I bared my baby
canines for Mam and Dad, showing off
the black embroidery, a tickle of stunned flies.

Dressing Up

They were difficult years. When I couldn't decide
if I wanted to be *Bunty* or *Jackie*.
Home from playing football on the rec, I'd dip
my hot toes in my sister's *Burnished Flame*.

The doodlebug hum of a long-dead war stung
in my mother's ears. Make-do was her *Dior*.
She'd come back from cleaning the chemist's
armed with Elizabeth Arden's cast-offs.

Deep brown velvet, rich and smooth as TV
chocolate. Fuchsia felt, sports car hip
and fab. Yards of lace, white as weddings.
A hollywood hoard of chiffons and satins.

Hands still fragrant with *Fairy* and *Ajax*,
she'd coax her treadle in two-steps,
fox-trots. The house was an iron orchestra
playing follow-my-leader, my mother's making.

I had to suffer the prick (*Keep still!*)
of the pins from her lips in my thighs
before the mirror would show me a *Linda*,
my new frock, fit for a queen, socks
bobbing a curtsey under medallioned knees.

Caracole

All my friends dreamed of a Pony Club heaven,
hosts of horses, well-groomed angels, chestnut,
roan, any nine-year-old girl would burn for.
Black Beauty left me frosty as a paddock
in winter. I never even had a bike.
But Paradise was Saturday night down
at the Labour Club, dashing white sergeants,
men in lipstick and sequins, stallion-eyed,
a clarinet playing *Moon River* over and over
until someone called Time switched the lights on
and everyone's face was yellow and singing.

The horses I liked were the ones at the front
my father backed, with thoroughbred names,
hooped and chequered jockeys and the flutter
of luck on their noses. I'd feel
their steaming breath quicken to silver
in my palm when Dad cantered home
from the bookies at tea-time.

And aren't I my father's daughter, a filly
who jumps and jumps and stays the course,
galloping across fields on a pony
I stole from a man named Shanks, putting
my shirt on the dazzle of chance,
no saddle, a loose rein?
And isn't heaven a saloon with plenty
of hooch and honky-tonk, flamingo women
singing like angels for all us gauchos
who'll go to bed with our boots on,
buckskin sun nuzzling the flat horizon?

Wisdom Teeth

I tongue the fossil whorl in the corner
of my aching jaw, try to paralyse
it into forgetfulness; remember
this same pain when Dad died. The other side.

My mouth is full of clawed shells, still growing,
even though my world's shrunk, my captains drowned.
This salty breaker I'm racked on, keening,
washes up dark treasure, wisdom I've found

in the wreck of lost lives. Like the morning
I trawled that small chalky box on the tiled
bathroom sill, to be caught in the yawning
of the top half of your ivory smile.

Mother's Ruin

After that wedding, I breathed the sour smell
of gin, you cradling the cold white bowl, light
ghosting frosted glass; Dad laughing as you groaned
over and over *I want to die, just want to die.*

Last month I heard you, from your bedroom, urge
yourself *Try! Try!* And then I found you,
dressed, waiting on the sofa, gasping louder
and louder, your eyes wild, your lips turning blue.

What can I do but douse these images
in stiff gins, relish the mad crack of ice,
lemon eyes, soothing savour of juniper?
No one to hear me crying *Why, why? Why?*

Her Father's Daughter

Smiling, he'd let me steal Saturday night sips
from his glass, big as a brimming barrel,
liquid mahogany, the colour of his eyes.
Now I drink my own and I'm seeing double,
bridges spanning years by the bottleful,
stars bouncing blue off the Tyne, pennies
burning holes in a little girl's hand,
her father smiling – my one and only.

Something for the Weekend

When the Tyne turns to silver, my dark dear,
won't we still taste the deep brown beer
on each other's lips, feel our heart's glass
soften with froth so we can't get enough?

Tonight I'll be your Tuxedo Princess,
drowning, dizzy, wet behind the ears,
in the arms of a star, the bringer of beers.

First Flight

Her mother's red suitcase is full of books;
its stiff black handle greases her tingling
fingers, her tight palm. It's good to check it

in, out, in, out. In the plane, the padded
grey cabin she's never seen from the outside:
a message on the wing warns her DO NOT

WALK BEYOND THIS POINT. But she's tap-dancing
out, in, out, in with how it might feel
to be a bird, an iron egg waiting

to crack in satin air. Take-off's a laugh
from her belly she can't keep *in, out, in,
out.* She's between two familiar strangers,

caught in her seat's smooth vinyl arms, the belt
cuddling the feathers tickling her stomach,
out, in, out, in. Then she's high and fearless,

drinking Lufthansa gin, *in, out, in, out.*
She wants to fling the windows wide and wave
the bloody sheets; one blue fledgling hour snatched

from her new utterly maculate life,
blown away like clouds of cut white flowers.
What she's lost isn't wings.

Some Like It Hot

Suddenly last summer's a modern times movie
and I'm a star. It's not Paris, Texas but life
is sweet as diamonds are forever under
the sheltering sky. I'm wild at heart, right on cue
like a cat on a streetcar named Desire.

Some like it hot and I like it hot

My basic instinct tunes in to distant voices,
still lives. The big chill thaws, gets steamy and flashes
the petrified forest forward to my big scene:

a brief encounter at a Manhattan cabaret
with some local hero who dances with wolves,
baiting his hook with arsenic and old lace.

Some like it hot and I like it hotter

I could go bananas on this rocky road. But
it's high noon and back to the future; another
take on the fatal attraction of hairspray
and high heels.

Some like it hot and I like it hottest

    As the long day closes, I'm Thelma
and Louise, I'm Betty Blue, I'm in bed
with Beetlejuice: a festival of flicks reeling
under my skin. Hellzapoppin'. This might be it,
the last picture show, point break. You only live twice.

Some like it hot and I like it hot as you like

Mae West on Furniture Polish

His rich mahogany does something to me,
horizontal, vertical and curved.
He makes me feel like a beautiful bird
perched on the arm of his settee.

When I saw my face reflected in
his gleaming gerandoles, I bid
with my heart and my credit card.
Now we live in rococo sin.

He's my Chip – Chip – Chippendale
and I'm his woman who does.

You know where you are with a chair,
arms always open; soft there,
hard here, all those special places where
it's just perfect, so exquisitely rare.

I prefer my fixtures and fittings to be
strong and silent, to look like money,
like they've got a past. I'm the envy
of all my friends.

He's my Chip – Chip – Chippendale
but I just call him Tom.

His French polishing, his chinoiserie
is something that feels quite new to me.
And what I do with a feather duster
gets us both in a fine-tooled fluster.

With his marquetry inlay and fretwork
he furnishes my every desire. I'm on fire
with all that burnished wood,
his ribbon-backed Neo-Gothic
more eloquent than words
can say. Our love is an antique room
I'm mistress of. We keep the curtains closed.

He's my Chip – Chip – Chippendale
and I'm his woman who does.

The Empress's New Clothes

The Milky Way's a casual drift of constellations,
confused as guests at a dinner party, slipped

through the grid of the table's symmetry.
On the other side of science, all she knows

is the size of chaos and she is nothing
but a displaced decimal point, an inflated balloon,

propelled into no end of dark, her world hurtling
out of control, a small globe spinning on an axis

thin as stretched wire. She has to write it
down, chart the drama of her own body, divide

her day into digestible acts – breakfast, lunch, dinner –
reducing her vision to the convex reflection

in the back of a spoon; her map of the universe,
an oblong mirror inside the wardrobe door;

her telescope telling two-dimensional lies she can't see
through: the flesh-coloured limits of her body,

arms and legs, she must inspect like an apprentice
commissioned to supply the perfect work of art.

From where she stands she can't catch the moon,
its rock, the cradle of its changes. Nor the plaque

on her door – a present from her parents – that paints
the shape of a child's name she's growing out of.

Falling for a dream of chic, she studied French,
as if another country might smother the nightmare

of home, a foreign language she could learn
from scratch, where everything matched,

a Chanel ensemble, packed into a patent purse,
square and black, swinging on a gilt chain.

She failed to account for the irregular verbs,
all those gallic curves, the cedillas of croissants,

coffee with cream. France was Sauce Béarnaise –
after the interval, she didn't stay for the second act;

had to invent her own. And once the strip-tease
started, there was no going back.

A model student, she ticked off her exams, grade-As
in Obsession, Abstinence and Subterfuge. Dad buried

himself in the Business Section; her mother served up
porridge, white bowls of mashed grains, her daughter

could only mash some more, stirring and stirring.
Under the table the dog was her furred accessory,

snaffling smuggled toast. And all she knew of the summer
were the miles of park and pavement she measured,

matching the dog step for step, the bite beneath her rib cage,
the swallow in her stomach dissolving into such a lean cleanness.

The season bright, light and sharp as a tooth;
a girl in bud, unfurling. The three guardians of her fate:

one, the dog, a spaniel called Tess (her surrogate mouth
and digestive tract); two, the wardrobe mirror,

a silver eye in her own image; and three, the scales –
see-saw surface she must walk, consult for daily auguries:

three low-life sweat-shop tailors with no taste,
spinning, weaving and cutting a trousseau

for a lost empress, her ashen back-cloth.
Too soon, too late, the tragedy was mis-cast.

She pulled the script in tight, like a belt, a tape measure,
weighed it on electronic scales so sensitive

they could tell you how heavy a feather is,
how much nourishment you can't live without.

All she took when she left home was one fat suitcase
stuffed to the seams with accumulated clutter,

in danger of bursting in public – her biggest fear –
the untidy trickle of crumpled cheap clothes, battered

menagerie of toys, notebooks written in code. She'd be revealed
as charlatan, ugly sister, ingénue, a mess of contradictions.

She kept the suitcase buckled up, her face refusing
to register the strain of its bulky weight.

Her daily bread was a game of chess,
strategies of attack and defence, played

on reassuring squares of black and white.
She was a grand mistress familiar with every gambit,

her cheekbones shining from the fight
like antique ivory rooks. Every Friday night out

with her friends, the best part of all was the prologue –
three hours bathing, anointing, brushing, painting,

a virgin sacrifice blessed by the mirror, its sybilline gaze.
In the third pub, after her third vodka and slimline,

something happened, something shifted out of joint.
The glowing row of lights on the red-flocked wall

suddenly changed into a chain of white skulls
dancing and grinning in time to the juke-box bass.

Squeezing past a haze of disembodied elbows and bellies,
she made it as far as the *Ladies* and only wanted

the one thing she was sure of, the dirty white bowl, to swallow
her up; to coil like a snake in the S-bend

and flush herself away. That was the first time –
with alcohol – then she couldn't keep anything down.

The irregular snack-size meals, they all came up, a thin bile.
The bathroom was her asylum, her shrinking white lie.

Without a struggle, the needle on the scales
nudged further back, piercing deeper thinner layers

of skin. She discovered a new world of new angles
and loved its raw-bone desert landscape;

fed her flaking skin generous helpings
of almond oil, cocoa butter, honey and oatmeal,

creamy concoctions too good to eat, her lips
chanting her contracted mantra: *thin, thin, thin, thin.*

The second harvest, she stopped bleeding, months
blurring into one long missed meal. Her secret,

her special sign: she was one of the elect,
living on air, kin of air and air she would become,

a perfect angel. Her angle to the rest of the world
spread into diminishing obliqueness.

How do you measure the angles of air, spiralling
like ghosts in and out of shifting horizontals?

How do you account for the absence of a single star,
the space it creates, pulsing, in its wake?

At the crematorium, the plain deal coffin was a surprise
of lightness, *barely heavier than a child's,*

men in dark suits were later heard to whisper.
Dispensing tea and Dundee cake, her mother's confession

of ignorance sends everyone home looking over
their shoulders, lead toxic in the pits of their stomachs.

In the snow-covered park the scattered ashes
settle, a fine grey galaxy of dust, melting

into nothing like monochrome, under a leafless beech.
Back at home they leave the ceramic name-plate

screwed on her bedroom door, slip the hand-written sign –
Do Not Disturb – inside the raided wardrobe,

before closing the winter-weight curtains against
the uncommonly acute light, white moon on white snow.

Pandora Akimbo

I don't believe in boxes. That was one
of Erasmus's Freudian cock-ups.
The only box is my body, its song
of milk, ambrosia too rich to sup.

My cornucopia was a red rag,
a locked horn. Brain-boxes like Hesiod
stake out skinfuls of history, pin tags
on women's bones; file us under God.

Pens and rapiers slip in sweaty hands.
One man's box is *pyxis*, is another
woman's *pithos*, her honeycomb vase; bands
of sweet white teeth sealed tight, smiling ajar.

The only boxes I keep are stacked hives
of bees that sting, at the cost of their lives.

A Little Thorn

O my love's like a little thorn
That pricks me so I bleed.
He thinks that I'm his darling rose;
But he's my garden weed.

It's just him and me and the sea;
So what's a girl to do
But spend all her long days dreaming.
But not, my love of you.

But not, my love, no, not of you,
Your whisky breath and tartan.
Unlike you, I have no rhymes
For the lips I dream of parting.

Next time you say goodbye, my love,
And kiss my ruby lips,
It might be the last time, my love:
I've suffered too many pricks.

Weighing the Heart

*Officially the heart
is oblong, muscular
and filled with longing.*
MIROSLAV HOLUB

*The way you love me is a house you've built
of thick stone with fires in every hearth
to warm me. The flames grow like orange flowers
out of black coal and so you sow your seed*

*in me. My lap is a patchwork apron
of photographs of our children, locked
together, like shiny mirrors, in a house
of thick stone, a place called home where the heart is.*

Every year is dangerous. There's always
no knowing. But the time is now that you
must weigh your heart to find out how much
it's worth. The time you find you love him

like a brother, like he's family, just because
he's there, a mountain you're too scared
to climb, where the air's too thin to breathe,
just enough to keep you alive, just enough

to hurt. The foothills on your map are riddled
with history, bullet holes and shifting
borders, traces of blood and little graves
with photographs and fading flowers:

a country of old campaigns. But the heart
is a history lesson you never learn
from. Try it as science instead: weigh it,
dissect it, list its various components.

Discover the truth. Record it. And find
the only heart you can measure is your own.
And once you start dividing it up, it gets
smaller and smaller till there's nothing left

to transplant. This part's for you and this part's
for you. *He loves me. He loves me not. He loves me…
not. And her. And her. And her.*
You're trying your best to walk straight ahead

but every day is another sharp corner
you catch yourself on, the limits of your body
defined by each new scratch and bruise.
You've lost your sense of direction. You're lost.

The map. Your heart. Discover the truth.
He loves you because he knows you so well.
He loves her because he hardly knows her
at all. Is that what the heart is? A mollusc

that doesn't know? An act of the imagination?
Beware the heart that commits a sexual
act. Beware the heart that knows nothing
but penetration, gets under your skin.

The body is a gift you can choose
to give. Or not. In equal measure.
Like your heart, tucked inside, its changing lights.
You are its brother, its keeper. You can not weigh

another's. You are not the keeper of your brother's
heart. But, like mirrors, the heart reflects and,
like rabbits, breeds. So before you know it, or
your heart, you have at least six to try not

to keep. Look at them all red and bloody
in the butcher's shop window. Balance them
on a silver scale. Your stomach will pay
the bill. Discover the truth. Record it.

The way you hurt me is a sitting-room
mirror smashed into fragments of silver.
You stick the shiny pieces onto the mantel
with strong glue. The edges cut your fingers.

You dip a brush in a pot of black paint
and write me a message. It doesn't say
'Welcome Home'. You're telling me the truth.
You love me. You promise. The lulling mantra

of the greedy, the desperate, cowards
who can't face the truth. *If I knew the truth*
I'd tell it you. I'd write it in big black
letters on the orange of the mantelpiece

and decorate it with glittering mirrors,
repeating it over and over.
I love you. I love you. I love you.
The heart like the camera never lies.

Here is a knife, sharp and cruel as the taunt of truth.
Use it to cut out your heart. Check it's still your own,
Kodachrome crimson and complete. *Don't lie*
to me. Ever. Tell me the truth. I don't want

to know what you did in bed. Don't tell me
that. Just tell me the truth. Record it.
The heart, like the camera, often lies,
tells its own version of many different truths.

He kisses my breasts and I see a picture
of hers. My heart's in there somewhere.
Like hers. Double bloom. Double exposure.
This bed's not big enough for all of us:

the telephones, letters, bunches of flowers,
the small, touching gifts, the stains on the sheets.
The bed's a fucking mess. And all I want
is clean linen, crisp, white, a good night's sleep.

He's had another letter. You know
by the way he tells you he loves you
over and over. He's written back. You know
because he buys you chocolate. You know

the rules of the game. Truth, dare or promise.
But now you're playing against the wind
and you can't see for tears. Your feet are cold
and wet. The sharp corners are tumbled bricks

of thick stone, broken promises. Your heart.
You're climbing the mountain whether you like it
or not. You have to see what's on the other side,
to find out if it's a better country,

greener grass. If you can manage without a map.
Your heart. The trek up is bog and rock.
Lichens grow like orange flowers, fragile, strong.
The light changes. Your feet are wet. You feel

the draught blowing through the space where your heart
should be. Weigh the air. Tell me. *The truth is,*
I have the heart of a hungry child
who's been given the key to a ruined house.

Spelling Home

What I wish for myself is a roof
that keeps out water, strong walls
to ward off cold, a fire to warm me.
These things are mine. I carry them
in the good house of my good heart.

I mix paints old and new to lighten
the rooms, restore the transparency
of windows. I've made a broom to sweep
away other people's dust I don't wish
to lodge between my toes. I walk

up and down wooden stairs, counting
each step, one at a time. I take
the hands of those I trust to help
me walk alone. My children sleep
the sleep of children in feather beds.

These things are mine. And I'm free
from the rattle at the door, someone
else's idea of interior décor, interesting
times that are no longer interesting.
Safe, I am, from the vagaries of weather.

The walls grow like healthy plants
and I rest easy in their green breathing.
Our rhythms match and make music.
I carry the key in the palm of my heart.
What I wish for myself is mine.

Acknowledged Land

(Northumberland, 10,000–700 BC)

One beginning is *cold*. It freezes our lips
like ice, hungry for the white of our bones.

Light and dark make shadows in the stretch of waking,
wild beasts of dreams that catch you in their teeth,

sweating under rancid skins, huddling for the warmth
of blood. This place here and now is only us,

more or less cold, stone chiselled from the silence
of winter. Even our fires are hungry, spitting

out orange snakes of heat; one half of us always
shivering. Flames tempt like lovers' eyes,

moons in black mirrors; leave you cold and sad
when you must rise with the sun and walk away

alone, another rampart raised around the settlement
of your heart. Every third child dies. We burn

the bones and make another mark in stone,
a cup of blood, a ring of milk. We are silted

with loss, morning frost on blades of grass, fine white
on, brave green; so many blades, knives

we whittle from the sharp sound of flint, dreaming
of words out of our lips' kenning, glinting

like the kiss of metal, a memory we've not forged
yet, can't forget. The moon keeps on, keeps on

turning into herself and back again. And so
do we, the year, freezing and melting.

No one remembers all the beginnings any more.
All we know is it keeps on happening.

*

We don't say second. What we wait for is *next*,
this, what, and after; try to remember

what came before, the shape it made in the sky,
the white abacus of stars, colour of days,

the texture of soil, grit of seed. The moon is our best
next, drawing us on, white as milk and good magic.

In her mirror we see the invisible becoming visible;
make her shapes with our mouths, our eyes,

our faces, build our safe places in the same way,
ring after ring of safe. We bracelet

our hearts; all her people, who want to live,
sow wheat and barley, in terraces of sense,

fields of healthy children whose faces
make the same shapes as ours, our eyes,

our mouths, the moon, their mother.
The women's bodies open into miracles, white

globes, and our children float down their rivers,
crying droplets of Os. We drink the blessing,

our hearts roaring. There are only two things we need
to know and they are one: what we need and

what is possible. We know these things are many.
Together they make grain and water in a clay bowl,

warmed in the glow of a fire, the good and round
in your belly, the come and go of your breathing.

The imaginary is only a thought that exists
to make something happen: come and come and go.

*

Here is a place where we are born, where our children
are born, where we and our children will die.

This place is where we live, the light
and shadows in between. We are people

breathing the green and purple of a vast land,
colonies of bees, beautiful, dangerous, orange

and black, feeding on honey. We choose high places
to build our homes. We hold up our heads, watch

31

horizons for changes in the weather, warning signs of danger.
Our foundations are strong shapes the earth makes, circles

we draw around ourselves, ring upon ring and stone
upon stone, beat back wild beasts, wilder weather.

From this hill top we can surrender, never stop
fighting. And what we see are more hills, mountains

capped in snow, greening in sunlight; rivers we call
Till or Tyne, winding like silver snakes, shedding

their skins in the dry: what time does over and over,
the great dissolver. The hill, the law of the land

is the lie of it we need to believe in since
this is the place where we are born. We call it

home; every day feel it touch the soft places
at the centre of our eyes, grateful

for its gift of good grain, fresh water, remember
its dangers; bury our dead beneath its thick brown

blanket, wind cutting the wet cheeks of those
left behind who must fight and surrender, stay safe.

*

Land of natural borders, rearing contours,
we watch them shift with the seasons, borrow

the shapes they make, find answers
to their questions. We acknowledge this land,

our debt to it, a pact of clasped hands,
the maps we carry on our open palms.

The spaces between cold and hungry and lost
we fill with the red of our blood,

our children and blessings. And so we make maps
of all our safe places, to remind us where they are,

how to find our way home in the dark. We carve
them out of the stone of our hearts, catch

the blood in crimson spirals, charting the gradient
of our country, the land where we live; know

how much geography we carry inside us, a home roaring
with rings of fire, oranges and blacks.

And all the places we know are safe, Old Bewick
and Dod Law, Yeavering Bell

and Lordenshaw, we see their names in lights,
beacons blazing gold under the silver-studded shield

of dark. In the cold, hungry and lost, they seem
to say we are not alone. We light fires

for each other in the dark. We are all
different and we are all the same; our skins,

our own natural borders, simply contours
exposed that need protection, feeding, warming.

*

Forest is menace, is mystery, a match fit
only for fools or the fearless. We don't know

which till after: either a deer to be skinned
and roasted, mead to be drunk, or just

an empty space round the fire at nights wearing
a fool's face. Water is also dangerous, gorgeous

with fish and flowing. Rivers are maps we can trace
the route of, follow up or down: to the place

where the water falls, a cauldron of earth and air
and this water, this Roughting Linn, a bull, bellowing.

And we bellow like bulls, spray fresh on our cheeks;
slake our thirsts and lift our heads. This place

is a special safe, holy days free of horizons,
a mirror of wisping prisms where we can see

our dreams dance and melt, what we need and what is
possible, what can be real. Whatever happens,

we go home with cleaner faces and lighter hearts,
strong as bulls, the red ball of the sun at our backs.

Beyond the borders of home in a grove of trees,
a rock lies sleeping. We sing it awake with rings

and cups, a wild garden of eyes. And sleeping,
dreaming, waking, stone outlives us all,

doesn't melt in fire or crumble in the fist
of weather. Its one surrender is to tricks of light.

So we play tricks too, make our mark on rock
with picks of stone, share the blisters.

*

Naming a thing is giving birth to it, a blessing
or a curse, an imaginary cloak of real power:

the magic works. The moon, its waxing and waning,
the women's blood, taught us that. We imagine

we want to hear the sounds of our own names, a word
like *the*, definite as granite, that always stays

the same. After a spell of thinking, it happens
and so we give birth to the name of the sun,

its power and glory. Though its heat may wax and wane,
the shape of its face stays the same. We want

to know the summer shapes our children's faces make
are the same as ours. We learnt that from the moon.

And still the women hold up half the sky
alone. Always changing, always bleeding, without

even the grace to die. So we name the sun
who knows what death really is, has power over life

and death, earth-scorching, thirst-making. Warriors
we are, hunters, who know the power and glory

of death. Our sun battles with the moon for the sky
and its strength splits day and night in two, a cracked egg,

yellow yolk, liquid white. One thought leads
to another and we dig our ditches deeper, raise

our ramparts higher, mine the earth and make metals,
copper, bronze and iron, our fires roaring.

Forging coins like little suns, we trade our lives
for seeds of ideas, with minds of their own.

34   *

Whatever we do, something new keeps on
happening, a new name. We etch alphabets

in wood or stone so we remember how we invented
the beginning of things, know the difference

between left and right, light and shade,
this man's wife, this man's son, and his neighbour's,

his enemy's: the lines we draw to divide
our territory. This is our land, the place where

we are born. We acknowledge it only with the brand
of our different names. There are many

uses of fire; blessing or curse, we imagine we know
the difference, kindling brittle sticks into orange

and black. Our skins grow coarse from the heat.
But we feel like gods and say it is good.

Only the earth keeps the silence of stone,
chanting its song of the seasons. We stop

our ears with wax, blind to our reflections
in other eyes. Too busy chasing the tail of time,

we never surrender, never stop fighting. Too busy
with the business of staying alive to know

what living is. We imagine this is vital and say it,
write it: it is *good*. Our hearts in their stockades

of one and one and one grow colder. Ice
splinters our blood, moon's not bold enough to melt.

We weave our stories into woollen cloth,
call our freedom *fate*. And the unravelling.

Sins of the Fathers

Inside him he kept chained a monster
that strained at its leash, troubled
by supplicants, intruders. What he couldn't
face were his own closed doors, the way
she could always make an answer for his
snarls, held the key to his barking.
It kept him keen, in his small régime,
its four walls, a roof with holes.
She had to wait for the rain to fall,
to wash away the blood from his biting.
He hit her, hit her, hit her, hit her
where it hurt; kept her chained
like a monster, who couldn't love himself,
the broken tendon in his heel.
In more than years she paid for
the scissors she used to cut the cord,
look him dead in the eye.
She said what she meant and meant
what she said: she didn't need him
to bleed, she said, didn't need him any more.

No Man's Land

Where is the country she's exploring: it has no borders.
Its name is edge. Neighbours march down her streets,
their soldiers' boots beating poisonous tattoos
in pursuit of cleansing, antiseptic illusion of enema.

Every exit is blocked with bodies, passport control.
The sky in her ears is streaked with the whine of jets,
blind to the planet's sacred anatomy of blood and bone.

She wanted to record history according to the facts,
thought the present was a safe stop en route to the future.
Until she saw the stains on her fingers from the ashes
of all the books they burnt. Then terror was the colour
of blood behind her eyes when the general punched her
after she'd screwed up the courage to tell him
how scared she was. She caught the crimson in her hands,
saw it drain away into the carpet, absorbing atrocities
like a camcorder on R & R. She's stuck in a gully
called Bliss/Paralysis. Her shoes are full of stones.

Out there is where the air is sour as the breath
of how many soldiers on orders to rape her, her
and her children. They have no map of their future.

One day at a time in an emergency. And the ambulances
with their engines doctored wail like women
in a classical tragedy, strident blue sirens, all eyes
and ears, open as wounds. There's something wrong
no one can put right, despite the U.N. Forces,
the designer diplomats. She's tried all the options.

But there's no new thing under the sun, its orange ball
of flame roaring its warning like a boy scout collecting
shillings in return for a badge his mother will stitch
on his sleeve before his arm is blown off in an incident
in the marketplace. His mother will be the last to be told.

She wished she'd stayed at home and watched it on television.
Sometimes she even thought she was. And was blood
really that red, the colour they used to mark borders.

Surfing on the S-Bahn

That's when I like it best, after dark,
    days best forgotten, nights shining
lights stretched in one long beautiful track,
    like a silver comet, a golden arrow shooting
red apples off a young son's head. Me
    and Tomas share a can of the strongest Pils
our rotten Marks'll run to. By the time we
    get to Tiergarten it's easy to be fearless.
All we've got is nothing to fear. And everyone
    sits there like dead people. Twitching
around the eyes. Too plucked chicken
    to utter a bloody useless word – when
we open the windows and doors – you feel it
    in your belly, a cold suck
of air drying the sweat on your hands. Lean out
    in the rushing spangled black

and you know there's no going back.

    The train's carrying you on its back
and you're climbing like a chimp clinging
    hand to hand foot to foot outside. It takes
a shot in slow motion until breathless, gasping,
    a hero, you reach the other door. Then
there's Tomas grinning, your greatest fan,
    to yank you in, shake your hand.
Christ, it feels so fucking good. So near someone
    else's death, you know you're really living.
And all the dead people's faces are masks
    of bourgeois scorn – something like laughing
in their white lips' yellow slackness.
    Corpses or cowards, it's the same thing
in the end. The train's travelling West
    and it's home to our mothers we're going
on the S-Bahn in the dark. That's when I like it best.

Protea Changes the Colours of the Duchy

Even now I don't know how I did it.
I passed my mother on the street and what she saw

was a man in a sea-green suit, a jaunty trilby
her daughter wouldn't be seen dead in.

My transformations convinced me home
was a wheel, the face of a clock, all the lovers

I don't regret. I eeled my way out of darkness.
The silver fish in my belly were an oracle to consult

for service, honour. Until my good behaviour
startled the bastards into shoals of disarray,

surrender. So when I met the boy, the future nudged
closer. Another wheel. I smoothed the bootprint

between his eyes. It melted in the maroon of my blood.
Never again would he suffer the affliction of safety.

The impossible certainty of success.
There I was, polishing his teeth like a fairy

with a pocketful of coins, sucking his sweetness
till my tongue tingled, watching his fish fleece.

I changed the colours of the Duchy and saw,
in that spot of ochre in his right iris,

my own face, changed, without the will to do it.
An ache like a distant volcano.

I, who thought I was the fisher, prophet, shepherd
of the seas, was caught on the mortal hook

of bliss, of not knowing what would happen next.
There's no telling what I will do.

Devorgilla's Sweet Heart

If this is death, I love it.
I am serenely decomposed,

his pickled heart in its armour
of gold besieging the beautiful bloom

of my Platonic left breast, caressed
by worms, good Galloway earth.

When white mists dredge themselves
from the sea, I slink between

the ginger ruins of arches, palms
poised in prayer. I watch those

who wear their National Trust cards
next to their hearts; indulge

in a little wager on those who'll last
as long as the gold on their fingers.

Sea thrift tongues a lesson in anatomy.
And I am proud of my heart's blood.

My eye's as clear as the sweetest mead,
reliable as the dog who stalks

the cloisters, fasting, every Friday night,
who howls at the mirror of the moon

for the abbey cat he loves
with every hair on his noble bones.

I will have words with that cat,
speak to her in malachite,

teach her the virtues of tapestry,
how to dance to the drum of the sea.

That's what I like about this death,
it's always *Auld Lang Syne*.

And isn't it always the ones who stay
at home who are the crusaders,

warriors of the heart.
Live forever.

The Spur in the Dish

First, there is this: the fine softness
of my children's skin I stroke and stroke
to blunt the iron of their absence.
Then this: the spur in the dish, a spike
in the tender place at the root of my throat.

The border gaol is a beacon of stone
guiding my young warriors home
after days in the hills reiving. I count
each brick, crush lichens into dust, fretting
over nothing but a spur in the dish.

This hungry ache is what time does left
to its own devices: plucks the petals
from daisies; weaves a ribbon of horses' hooves.
Border warfare leaves a bruise; my heel, a blue
and gold fleur-de-lys when I remove my shoes.

Everyman's Blues

If you will be my queen, crown me King of Fools.
You dance in Egyptian, emerald fire faceting

your thighs. So I smoulder like a land at war
for one hundred years; my blood, the beat of your

tambourine. You are my white candle burning
for Our Lady, though I know you discourse with goats.

Your magic is marble and shadow; your tears,
the only art you need. I want to be your goat,

your Gutenberg, your blue, blue lake. Aren't you a child
who's lost her shoes, a half-moon rising in the sky

to take up arms with that soldier, the sun?

All things to all men, a woman like you
could ruin a man. If he's lucky. I want

to be lucky; want to taste your bowl of honey,
sting of a thousand bees. I am a pig, roasting

on a spit, a bear on a chain. You've got me
by the throat, the mark of the Devil on my hands.

You are an Act of God. With my one good eye,
my cloth ears, I need the blessing of your breasts,

angelus bells; beneath your skirt, the petals
of a rose. Watch how I'll cut your purse, sentence

you to death to show you what justice isn't.

Bruising the Sky

I

A day in May beginning
with rain, blossom sticking to
slick grey streets like postage stamps.
The journalist's wife hid

a linen envelope behind
the toaster till the wings
of his jacket lifted him
to work, a dry kiss dropped

on her forehead. She already
felt the eight legs of the spider
script crawl between her thighs. *Filth.*
Check it out. Her secret shadow

spun around the house unravelling
cobwebs; danced on carpets
of petals and forgot to buy
the milk, what to do in

emergencies, *Mayday, Mayday.*

II

There's a certain point where blue becomes brown,
the way day slips into twilight into
evening, like a man taking off his shoes,
loosening the tie round his neck,
a limp star on the sofa, still not paid for.

No one was available to give me
an interview so I'm making this up.
As good as all those other lies. Read all
about it, the little of the all of the it
they'll let us have. No doubt about it.

It's all bad for you, seeps into
your pores till you find yourself looking
at the cherry blossom and wondering
if its baby pink is a confetti
of lies, this spring nothing more than a haze
that is sometimes blue, that is sometimes brown.

Somebody's not telling us something and
I want to know his name, see the colour
of his money when it falls like confetti
through this thick air nobody wants to breathe.
Our nostrils, our lungs feel uneasy,
like strangers at a wedding, afraid
to take another glass of sherry.

III

The playground's a nest of cracking
voices, ropes turning, hair streaming,
tracks in toxic coral.
An early bell hauls the children

in, where they must remove their shoes,
not trail a wake of dusty silt
every fourth child will swallow,
biting back breath; that no one

will name but leaves its mark
in the register: a thin
absent *O*, an anxious note
on blue paper, the doctor's name.

IV

A weed is only a plant growing in
the wrong part of the garden. Swear softly,
root it out; fingernails waxing black moons.

Their buts, althoughs, howevers are pillars
of smoke. How do you kill something that's dead
already? And who of us can bury it alone?

V

What little light there is leans
down to touch the people's skins,
feels like rain they'll wash away.

The journalist's wife is velvet,
is river, scudded with not quite
the right words at the right time.

Spiders drown in her waters.
She breathes crimson air, thorns.
Inside her belly a baby

is growing, a little frog
that will fall out of the sky
like light, like rain, looking for

Daddy. Her husband nurses
his wailing words in quilts
of print, rain dotting and dashing.

VI

That by-line will be the death of me,
but I don't want a job that's cowardice,
that's Pravda. *Silence is sometimes yellow,*
not the precious gold I know I'm risking.

What colour are the right words? How do I say
'Why do your eyes always look to the left
of me so I can't see if they're blue
or brown? And what's that new scent, licking

your wrists, the secret place behind your ears,
an expensive smoky citrus?' She used
to smell of roses, an English garden
in summer, her eyes blue as cornflowers.

VII

In the dark no one is brave enough
to say *it is this* or *it is that*,
the bruise of what is true.
                              In the dark
the billows of blue are white; base metal
reek of phenol, smudged ink.

And isn't everyone doing their best, running
out of words, like *betrayal*, like *breath*?

In 1991 D. of E. guidelines set the recommended limit for formaldehyde
emissions at 20mg per cubic metre of air. The Egger chipboard factory in
Hexham produces up to 142mg; as well as particulates and volatile chemical
compounds three times in excess of recommendations.

Airhead

I knew one once. He was that far gone
he took it as a compliment, padding
his brain's blank spaces with psychedelic
graphics, cool as seraphic cadillacs, sweet
as angel cunt.

Hard to tell when the pollution started. One day
he woke up screaming *Mommy!* And wasn't she
always there watching over him like his own
third eye, myopic? He didn't know whether
to love her

or hate her. He thought she was a thistle
he could ack-ack-ack or nap-nap-napalm.
He thought thistles were beautiful, needed
the stitch of their silver prickles. But
she never died.

She grew back in the black air behind
his little boy blue eyes. She was a creature
of many incarnations, he observed cross-legged,
playing at Krishna, in love with Kali.
He broke all

the strings of his guitar, singing himself
to sleep at nights, cuddling his purple-crested god.
And it crowed three times every morning
in some poor cow's yard. The air inside
his head smelled

of farm, of fire, of fuck. He hummed
the mantra *love* over and over. And all it was
in fact was chemistry, potent, lethal,
nothing but air.

The Eater of Wives

Call me old-fashioned, but I'm never mean
with saffron. How many times have I heard
my own grandmother say the man who's tired
of good food, cooked with love, is a man dying?

Mornings, it's true, I'm moody and blinking
before I dress my eyes with the fragrant scales
of fish. I gave up meat years ago. God knows,

it's taken me forty years to feel this
restless, spicing my hollow nights with women
who taste like apples, cherries, pears. I eat out
in every town. And the little lady
at home feeds me her pretzel arms, her marzipan arse.

I hate sleeping in the shell of my own breath
so I follow the raw scent of my sweat,

what's cooking between their legs; suck them dry
as cocktail martinis till my head spins
with their names. *Charlotte. Rosemary. Hélène.*

I just pick up the phone; hear my voice saying
Remember me? bubbling like a thick soup
of oysters and mussels from the Bay
of Angels. Listen, all I want is the best, some
girl who'll eat me back, lick the plate clean.

In the Waiting Room

Consult your tongue like a weather forecast,
a satellite of spores. Your eyes, lupine,
change colour according to the phases
of the moon. Regret the gaps in your
knowledge of iridology. Your skin
is a suit of sandpaper inside out,
ticklish as hell. Like the morning cough that
lasts as long as the words *tuberculosis,
bronchial pneumonia, emphysema,*
flowers rotting on the stems of your lungs.

Every night at 4 a.m. you wake to
a black bruise, a tinnitus of birds
needling the air: dream of the child you were,
packed off to school, bleeding, burning, without
a note. Every day you choose the manner
of your own death, like someone cruising
a department store, seeking a vital
electric appliance they will pay for
with a gold card. Only then will you
be happy. And your hands might stop
their shaking, jittering on invisible
wires, your symptoms cease to breed, brittle as locusts,
flailing their wings beneath your alopecia.

Admit it. Your bedside reading is Gray's
Anatomy, A Short History   .
of Decay: the prognosis, a minty
white placebo spinning out of orbit.

Meteorology

Afterwards she blamed it on the wind, cold
in the air like someone's breath in her ear.
And listening was the mistake she made,
wishing its wild stories were really true.
The almanac they consulted lied,
its wicked lips closing and opening,
an oracle of storms, mercury trapped
in blue glass. And afterwards that something
had happened, something beginning with *m*,
was all she knew, that tasted like the wind,
smoke and citrus, someone else's perfume.
The weather changed: something lost, something gained,
the rain, filled the space between them, so far
apart, buckets and buckets of weather.

Taking Me from Behind

Friday's moon, its white smile irising
the sky in my belly, is the way
you whispered *Baby* and rocked me
with your hips. That kiss

goodbye at the station, minding the gap
between trains, tongued this strange hiatus
before need bites desire; stopped
the mouths of two

babies crying. And I'm shunting in
and out of what blue eyes do, coupling
the sear of green; how by now you've eased
your skin into other skies

and the ache in my thighs is missing
you. My pelvis is a cat's cradle,
stringed with old guitars. Your face
is dark as a demon's:

what right hands do when the left's not
looking, on top and under. Best
was behind and sideways and during,
a collision so surprising,

so back to front, I'll wonder later:
if we ever, what on earth. Watch me
lower the creases we made into
orchids; still the scent of you

my hungry mouth can't name without thinking
of a bird, utterly earthed migrations.

Guilty as Sin

If you held a thin felt-tip in those soft fingers
I recognised as artistic and joined up all
the moles and freckles that dot my body,
could you draft me a map of the heavens?

Once in Amsterdam I made love on a roof
with an angel. Afterwards, side by side,
our hands made lace wings, eyes sieving
silver perforations of sky, quilt
enough in the burn of waxed feathers.

I'm only telling you this because I know
your southern hemisphere is a spinning mirror.
See, on my cheek, flying home, there's
a single swan, of which I am vain, lifting
my chin, the way I did to raid the nest
of your lips. If that were my only sin.

Truly, I'm trying to ground this starry tyranny:
I levitate, get lost in space, spawn
holograms of seraphim playing merry hell.
At least this equinox I divined you might bring
a sting, a carapace I couldn't pierce. Unlike
your fingers massaging the soft spot on my neck,
a constellation you recognised as *Guilt*.

Doing It Right

'Apollonius to Zeno, greeting. You did right to send the chickpeas to Memphis. Farewell.'

It's at times like this you know there's nothing
else to do but send the chickpeas to Memphis.

Miles Davis only makes it worse, doing
a Theseus through the slug pellets around

your emotions. Where you are is up
Jacob's Creek, soft and fruity with good length

and an acid finish. The only
messages on your machine are from some

guy called Apollonius. You might meet
him one day. Don't mention his mother.

All you want is to do it good, do it
right. You stoop to consulting the horoscope

in the *Radio Times*. I ask you,
does it help? Do giraffes drive around town

in limousines? Does the summer triangle
look like a geometry lesson? Vega,

Deneb, Altair: a swan with a lyre
wooing an eagle. The words you least want

to hear – *it is not possible*. There must
be a book in a library out there

somewhere with all the answers between
its covers. You know it's not called *What is*

Emotion? And it's got nothing whatsoever
to do with zoos. Or Michelangelo's

David. Too much to do with anarchy
and that damn moon I'm planning never to

speak to again. Don't even consider
what would happen if the spider crawling

up the centaur's legs, mistaking him for
a giraffe, spun a web around his balls

to catch a better view of the stars,
the summer triangle, Vega, Deneb,

Altair, and wherever the hell the moon
is, getting it all on video. Don't

regret a thing. Send the chickpeas to
Memphis and only think of the harvest.

The Gentleness of the Very Tall

(after Chagall's 'La Maison Rouge')

Even the tallest didn't remember
Napoleon saying *Let them eat leaves.*
Each bite of apricot moon teased hunger,

buttery and forgetful, a dark stone
for a heart gritting its little white pip
of heaven. Despite their facility
for sleight and coaxing, hands just can't manage

pollination by air. One finger might
journey the curve of a thigh or a scythe,
the white of one eye. Or two. Isn't
any the wiser, though soothed by simply

moving, at least the possibility
of gentleness. Why else feel air thinning
with altitude, with the brassy sound

of a very beautiful musical
instrument, what happens to heat when
silence rises. And never ends. Even
when the tallest must climb up trees to see

the sun and the moon shine together
in the sky over red rooftops, quite
a small woman breathing mists on a mirror,
seeding oceans: storms, tranquillity, nectar.

Medicine Woman

The attic sky is a sleeping green heart.
You've left your winter carapace at the door;
trace the kite of Auriga, the sturdy scent

of sage. The little pot-bellied stove warms
you with all the comfort of Bavaria,
gingerbread you'll chew to keep you from harm.

She brings terracotta pots, thumbed with lace,
to catch the salt water that melts from your
eyes, down the stone mountain that is your face.

And your breasts billow into doves of air.
She coaxes you alight with the coals at
the centre of her eyes; her hands, a small

cathedral in her lap, catch the rattle
of your dark. She unwraps a velvet mirage,
marked on the map by a charm of metal.

Here you will see your wounds are fans, large
and satin, you can open or close. And
you will survive, as a snake does. Forever.

For one hour, over and over, she can
be all the mothers you never had, all
the daughters you'll never carry, your sons.

She gives you, idiot child, an egg you'll
swaddle in the twisted silk of your hair.
Like a rope she rises, like a rope pulled

away. You are naked as a peeled pear.
She eats you till you are just pips that will
sprout in loam, the luxury of your tears.

Body Language

...metaphors are dangerous. Metaphors are not to be trifled with.
A single metaphor can give birth to love.
MILAN KUNDERA

Before, she used to need a translator
to understand what his body language
signified, its present tense. She declined
the metaphor of eye contact, explored
the academic use of pseudonym.

Why is the alphabet in that order?
was one of many unsettling questions
provoked by the microfiche of letters,
dinner, too much whiskey. Bed was always
conditional; might be superlative.

When the VDU bleated *Insert, Text,*
Merge, she couldn't process the words on the tip
of her tongue, nipple, hip, solar plexus,
clitoris: the cowardice of one who
knew what systole meant, diastole, oscillation.

Striping the Sheep

It's better to be a tiger for one day than a sheep for a thousand years.
INDIAN PROVERB

You will know something is happening
when a small rectangular thought melts

and swivels into a black diamond
that sucks all the light there is

into the faceted mirror of its shadow.
Less than a second later the grass

pricks up its ears at the vegetable
dipthong of a baa chewing a growl,

stripping it back to a roar
which spikes not only chlorophyll. Proof

that the food chain is a rural myth.
Muscles adopt the concept of haunch

and sinew and bone forget tomorrow.
Lanolin ignites into orange

and black, an attitude of fur. So Pure
New Wool is an atavistic memory

in the mind of a creature wreaking havoc
somewhere in Bengal. Not Good Old Blighty.

You will know you were born
the best sort of bastard, really living.

Zoology Is Destiny

You won't let me be ostrich, armadillo,
invertebrate. Although for you I'm zoo,
a new creature, prowling behind bars, howling
at the moon, the way you can stroke the hairs
riding the roaring switchback of my spine –
a terrible gesture of tenderness.

If I can't come out, you'll come in – pick
the lock on the door of my cage with your teeth.
We dine on watermelon and figs, milk
and almonds, our tongues cunning as Eden snakes.
Our hands build an ark, two by two, for fur,
feathers flying, hoof, breastbone, muzzle, wing.

This is not a parable wishing itself
would happen, like weather in a fable
by Aesop, a date in *The Fox and Grapes*.
It's simply the vatic utterance
of a white rhinoceros who knows
the difference between rocks and crocodiles.

Clouded Leopard

In the dip of a branch spooning the sky
dry wood licks the perilous curve of fur,
nutmeg-speckled milk, a cirrus of eyes.

The civet smell of home gives the caged air
an appetite for solitude, the blue
certainty of sky, spilt on root and trunk.

This sleeping cat's tail is a question mark
upside down, a bell rope muzzling the sound
of breathing padding its paws in my throat.

Still life unpeels in a yawn like a saw
and where there should be a leg there's only
the shock of nothing at all, a black spot

mirroring obsidian in my eyes:
a wound you failed to notice from behind
the strange transparency of your lenses.

Cowbound Lane

In Lunedale we're learning a new cartography.
A lowing herd of two, what we're studying is
bovine geography, milking the borders
of udder and tongue. My hooves are numb and pink; you
grow horns in new black leather. The grass we're grazing
can't resist this winter weather. The enormous sky
loses us under its belly of butter. But still
we thread the haystack-needle of Cowbound Lane.

It goads us down through marsh and rock, past sitka spruce.
You stop to snort and I lick your cheek's warm hide.
The map we're making is home, ordnance of the wild,
the dairy, the domestic. Back at the barn,
I bring milk to the boil. We lap it up and doze.
Till our eyes rise like moons, lips smudge contours that scale
a white siring. Both of us, ruminating
creatures, who'll not be bound by our own beaten tracks.

Antojito

Five thousand miles from Mexico, I'm your
señorita, compañero I've known
more than five thousand years. My big boots click

under the chair legs and my face pinks from
the candle's glow. We order in Spanish,
bold as colts, talk about fire while we wait,

drinking the Americas, sangría,
Sol, with a tiny slice of lime you bruise
in your tall glass. Your fajita comes to

the tile-topped table sizzling, aubergines,
chickpeas, jalapeno peppers and cheese.
My guacamole salad is served in

a burrito. I need a siesta
before I've eaten half. Whatever
passes between our hungry lips, it will

always be antojito, a little
whim, whatever we fancy. When we leave,
the crescent moon is sliced white tomato

shining down on our hot spicy bellies,
going home to sip cool margaritas
in my bandit of a bed, Mexico.

Intoxicated with Firs
(after Neruda)

Intoxicated with firs, unfolding kisses,
I coax the full sails of roses, like summer,
leaning into day's dying breath,
drowning in a thick fret of ocean.

Struggling to crest that hungry water,
I drift in the acrid air of raw weather,
silted with sounds like *grey*, like *sour*,
and the drenched manes of lost white horses.

Wild with love, I'm riding a single wave,
the moon, the sun, in flames, on ice:
moored in the welcome hollow of islands,
cool and soothing as pale hips.

My skin of kisses shivers on starry pillows,
electrified to the pitch of madness,
sparking desire, like some hero
getting drunk on early roses.

Till further, deeper down the waves,
your body is my body; melts in my arms
like a fish I'll always catch,
in and out, the quick breath of the sky.

High Time

You always wanted to play *Who's tallest*,
calibrating hip to hip, eye to eye,
lip to lip. Gauging its strange importance,
I'd always let you win. Much later, we stood back
to back, and the hover of hands was left
to crest the right answer. You had your sights
set on a heaven that gave me vertigo.
But five hundred feet above sea level, we
both grew, twin pillars with a faulty arch,
stone and salt, catching the rise of the wind.

Now, standing face to face, you ask me if
I've grown, lifting your blue to my hazel;
the span of your hands, the breath of the stove
on my back. I kiss your neck like a bird,
measuring the distance. We compare heels.
But nothing can account for the three inches
I seem to have gained in the year since
we parted. Nothing but the time it took,
incalculable, horizontal, for me
to grow into myself, taller, soaring.

Raising the Roof

Fish die belly-upward and rise to the surface; it is their way of falling.
ANDRÉ GIDE

Think about it: fish is the opposite
    of elephant, consigned to a life-time
of cold-blooded amnesia; until the night comes
    it must wink its eye at a mouth that will
eat it. Walk past the fish shop, orange, pink,

and silver, full of fallen fish. Think like
    a pachyderm, think of ahimsa,
the devilment of hooks. Remember
    that rumour of the woman who fell from
a window she mistook for a door

and swam through the air like a salmon
    coming home to spawn. What she was doing
was raising the roof. High enough for her
    to fall. A diver with wings, angel fish.
But how she landed was belly-down, path

punching her breath, filleting her pelvis;
    the liquid memory of breast-stroke,
butterfly. A siren shoal saved her the only
    way they knew how: wouldn't let her rest, swivel,
so her belly could surrender to the salt

lick of the sky; sun, a stone in her navel.
    Recall the curse of the fish, those gentle ones
who see and swim in circles, scales of light,
    who forget they're not ready to fall:
more roofs to be raised; more surfaces plumbed.